U.S. Department of Justice
Office of Justice Programs
Office of Juvenile Justice and Delinquency Prevention

J. Robert Flores, Administrator · Juvenile Justice Practices Series

JUVENILE JUSTICE BULLETIN

June 2004

Access to Counsel

Judith B. Jones

The Office of Juvenile Justice and Delinquency Prevention (OJJDP) is presenting a Juvenile Justice Practices Series to provide the field with updated research, promising practices, and tools for a variety of juvenile justice areas. These Bulletins are important resources for youth-serving professionals involved in developing and adopting juvenile justice policies and programs, regardless of their funding sources.

This second Bulletin in the series examines access to legal counsel in the juvenile justice system.

OJJDP supports the development and adoption of policies and programs that:

◆ Provide access to quality (not cursory) legal counsel for all youth in the juvenile justice system.

◆ Ensure that juveniles consult with counsel at the outset of the juvenile justice process (before waiving their right to counsel) and at every subsequent step, through postdisposition.

The right to counsel for juveniles was established in 1967 with the landmark case *In re Gault*, 387 U.S. 1, 87 S. Ct. 1428 (1967). In *Gault*, Supreme Court Justice Abe Fortas wrote, "under our Constitution the condition of being a boy does not justify a kangaroo court," and the Court ruled against the argument that a probation officer or judge could adequately represent a minor, given the "awesome prospect" of incarceration until the age of majority. The Supreme Court held in *Gault* that children have the right to remain silent and that no child can be convicted unless compelling evidence is presented in court, under the due process clause of the 14th amendment. *Gault* was a major change in juvenile law in that it upheld the constitutional rights of children. As Justice Fortas wrote: "Neither the 14th amendment nor the Bill of Rights is for adults only." The 6th amendment also protects children's rights to assistance of defense counsel (*Gideon* v. *Wainwright*, 372 U.S. 335 (1963)) and, moreover, to *effective* assistance of counsel (*Stickland* v. *Washington*, 466 U.S. 668 (1984)). The 6th and 14th amendments, along with the privileges enumerated in the Bill of Rights, form the constitutional lexicon of juvenile justice.

In response to *Gault* and other decisions affecting juveniles and to concerns about the treatment of youth in the justice system, Congress enacted the Juvenile Justice and Delinquency Prevention Act in 1974 (42 U.S.C. § 5601 *et seq.*, Public Law 93–415). The Act created the National Advisory Committee for Juvenile Justice and Delinquency Prevention, which was charged with developing a set of national juvenile justice standards. The resulting Institute for Judicial Administration-American

Bar Association (IJA-ABA) *Juvenile Justice Standards* (IJA-ABA, 1980) included a requirement that juveniles must be represented by counsel from the earliest stages of the court process. Yet research continues to show significant variation among states and within counties regarding effective assistance of counsel and commitment to indigent juvenile defense.

This Bulletin describes issues surrounding legal counsel in the juvenile justice system, explores factors that hinder access to and quality of counsel, discusses the elements of quality counsel, and offers examples of how some states and local organizations are meeting the challenge of improving access to legal counsel for juveniles. The Bulletin also includes a list of resources and tools for practitioners.

Issues Surrounding Legal Counsel in the Juvenile Justice System

The American legal system is complex. It is based on constitutionally guaranteed rights, common law precedent, and a web of federal and state statutes, local ordinances, and procedural rules. Mounting an adequate defense in juvenile or criminal court, avoiding self-incrimination, and ensuring that rights are upheld require the assistance of competent legal counsel. Yet many minors who become involved with the juvenile justice system never realize these basic rights because they ill-advisedly waive their right to counsel, inappropriately accept plea bargains, or receive substandard services. In some jurisdictions, as many as 80 to 90 percent of youth waive their right to an attorney because they do not know the meaning of the word "waive" or understand its consequences. Inadequate access to quality ancillary services—mental health, health, social, and educational—exacerbates the problems for defense counsel who are hard pressed to argue for nonexistent alternatives to detention and incarceration.

The path through the juvenile justice system begins with arrest and continues through postdisposition. At all points in the process, counsel must intervene effectively and zealously to ensure that youth receive the services they need to forestall future encounters with the juvenile justice system and that confinement is reserved for only appropriate cases. The following step-by-step review of the process calls attention to evidence that juveniles often do not receive this kind of consistent, effective legal representation.

Arrest and Detention

A juvenile first comes into contact with the juvenile justice system at the time of arrest. At that point, police have the discretion to release the youth with a warning or to conclude that evidence is insufficient to hold the youth for further processing. If a case proceeds, the juvenile is either released to his or her parents or guardians or sent to a detention facility.[1] In some jurisdictions, appointment of counsel for arrested youth may not take place until the youth appears in court.

After arrest, a detention hearing is held to determine whether the juvenile should remain confined prior to adjudication. The timeframe for this hearing is set by state statute; most take place within 24 hours of arrest. According to Puritz et al. (1995), citing 1992 data (Butts, 1994:5–6), a disposition of incarceration is more likely for juveniles who are detained prior to adjudication than for those who are returned to their families or placed in an alternative, community-based program. Other data indicate that the relationship between detention and likelihood of incarceration has a disproportionately large effect on youth from poor, minority, and single-parent families (Leiber and Stairs, 1999:68). During every year between 1990 and 1999, black juveniles were more likely to be detained than white

---

[1]Juveniles were detained in 20 percent of the nearly 1.7 million cases processed in 1999 (Harms, 2003).

Research on the Status of Access to Legal Counsel for Juveniles

The Bulletin's discussion of issues surrounding access to counsel and factors that hinder access to and quality of counsel draws on the major research studies described below.

National Studies

A Call for Justice: An Assessment of Access to Counsel and Quality of Representation in Delinquency Proceedings (Puritz et al., 1995). This report documents findings from a national study by the ABA Juvenile Justice Center that included a survey of public defenders' offices, court-appointed attorneys, law school clinics, and children's law centers; interviews with judges, defense attorneys, prosecutors, clients, court administrators, and youth advocates; and site visits to juvenile detention and corrections facilities.

Juvenile Justice Representation Rates Varied as Did Counsel's Impact on Court Outcomes (U.S. Government Accounting Office, 1995). In this national study, researchers surveyed prosecutors and interviewed judges to learn their perceptions of the quality of defense counsel for juveniles.

State Studies

The state study reports listed below were published by the ABA Juvenile Justice Center in association with juvenile advocacy organizations. Researchers who conducted the state studies surveyed and interviewed attorneys, judges, juvenile court personnel, youth and their parents, and youth advocates.

Georgia. *Georgia: An Assessment of Access to Counsel and Quality of Representation in Delinquency Proceedings* (Puritz and Sun, 2001).

Kentucky. *Kentucky: Advancing Justice: An Assessment of Access to Counsel and Quality of Representation in Delinquency Proceedings* (Puritz and Brooks, 2002).

Louisiana. *The Children Left Behind: An Assessment of Access to Counsel and Quality of Representation in Delinquency Proceedings in Louisiana* (Celeste, 2001).

Maine. *Maine: An Assessment of Access to Counsel and Quality of Representation in Delinquency Proceedings* (American Bar Association Juvenile Justice Center and New England Juvenile Defender Center, 2003).

Maryland. *Maryland: An Assessment of Access to Counsel and Quality of Representation in Delinquency Proceedings* (Cumming et al., 2003).

Montana. *Montana: An Assessment of Access to Counsel and Quality of Representation in Delinquency Proceedings* (Albin et al., 2003).

North Carolina. *North Carolina: An Assessment of Access to Counsel and Quality of Representation in Delinquency Proceedings* (Grindall, 2003).

Ohio. *Justice Cut Short: An Assessment of Access to Counsel and Quality of Representation in Delinquency Proceedings in Ohio* (Brooks and Kamine, 2003).

Pennsylvania. *Pennsylvania: An Assessment of Access to Counsel and Quality of Representation in Delinquency Proceedings* (Miller-Wilson, 2003).

Texas. *Selling Justice Short, Juvenile Indigent Defense in Texas* (Stewart et al., 2000).

Virginia. *Virginia: An Assessment of Access to Counsel and Quality of Representation in Delinquency Proceedings* (Puritz, Scali, and Picou, 2002).

Washington. *Washington: An Assessment of Access to Counsel and Quality of Representation in Delinquency Proceedings* (Calvin, 2003).

ABA Juvenile Justice Center staff and their professional colleagues in the field are currently conducting state-by-state research on the status of access to legal counsel for juveniles. The goal of this research is to identify systemic issues in all 50 states, with a view toward providing information to state legislatures and executive branches and, ultimately, improving access to counsel through state-specific systems change.

juveniles, for all offense categories (Harms, 2003). Although the U.S. Supreme Court (*Schall* v. *Martin*, 467 U.S. 253 (1984)) ruled that pretrial detention can be used not as punishment but only to protect the child and the community, surveys in many states found that youth are routinely and inappropriately sent into detention. Youth may be detained as a "scare tactic" or to accommodate court calendars. Furthermore, if counsel does not meet the client until the detention hearing, the attorney cannot effectively investigate placement with a relative or other community-based alternatives.

Effective representation at the earliest stages can have important effects on the outcome of a case. An attorney who talks to a client immediately after arrest can:

♦ Learn about any conversations the youth may have with police, intake workers, and family.

♦ Explain the process and ensure that the youth does not inappropriately waive the right to counsel, admit guilt, or make other detrimental statements or decisions.

♦ Quickly identify people who are in a position to speak well of the youth (e.g., teachers, ministers) and ask them to testify on the youth's behalf.

♦ Provide the detention hearing judge with enough information (e.g., family strengths, possibility of placement with extended family, or other alternatives to detention) to warrant release rather than detention.

Pretrial

Investigation. During the pretrial phase, the attorney investigates the facts of the case and files pretrial motions on behalf of the client. *Juvenile Justice Standards* (IJA-ABA, 1980) stipulates that the attorney should meet with the client and begin investigating as soon as possible, when memories are fresh and witnesses are relatively easy to find. *Standards* also instructs defense attorneys to obtain information from police, prosecutors, schools, probation, family members, and child welfare as soon as possible. Often, however, the amount of time an attorney can allocate to conducting investigations and learning about a client and case is insufficient to mount an adequate defense (see "Factors That Hinder Access to and Quality of Juvenile Defense Counsel," page 6).

Hearing for waiver or transfer to criminal court. The pretrial phase may involve a hearing to determine whether a juvenile's case should be heard in criminal (i.e., adult) court. During the 1990s, 49 states and the District of Columbia passed statutes that make it easier to prosecute juveniles in adult courts (Cumming et al., 2003, citing Redding, 2003). In most states, transfer (also called waiver) to adult court is automatic, depending on the age of the juvenile and the seriousness of the offense. If transfer is not automatic, however, the prosecutor must make a *prima facie* case, showing probable cause that the juvenile's crime is serious enough to warrant transfer and that the juvenile will not respond to treatment within the juvenile justice system (IJA-ABA, 1980). The defense attorney's responsibility is to argue against transfer and to keep the case in the juvenile court.[2] Research findings underscore the importance of effective and zealous representation for juveniles in waiver hearings.[3]

---

[2]In 1990, approximately 7,500 cases—less than 1 percent of the 962,000 formally processed delinquency cases—were waived to adult court (Puzzanchera, 2003).

[3]The Sentencing Project (a national organization that supports alternatives to incarceration) reports that juveniles prosecuted in adult courts include a disproportionate number of minorities and a high percentage of abused children and children who are mentally or educationally limited (Poe-Yamagata and Jones, 2000; Young, 2000).

OJJDP data show that although the number of judicially waived cases involving black youth decreased 24 percent between 1990 and 1999 while the number involving white youth increased, black youth still accounted for 44 percent of total cases waived in 1999 (Puzzanchera, 2003). In Florida, a study by the Office of Program Policy Analysis and Government Accountability found that juveniles in the adult prison system were almost 21 times more likely to be assaulted or injured than those in the state's juvenile facilities (Greene and Dougherty, 2001). Another study reported that, compared with adult inmates, youth in adult facilities are eight times as likely to commit suicide, five times as likely to be sexually assaulted, and almost twice as likely to be attacked with a weapon by inmates or beaten by staff (Cumming et al, 2003, citing Redding, 2003).

Findings such as these suggest the possible consequences of ineffective representation in waiver hearings. To argue effectively that a juvenile should not be detained (or ultimately incarcerated) with adults and can be rehabilitated within the juvenile justice system, a defense attorney must gather supportive information about the youth's social, educational, and family history. Often, however, insufficient time and resources are available to conduct a thorough investigation (see "Factors That Hinder Access to and Quality of Juvenile Defense Counsel," page 6).

Adjudication

The adjudication hearing parallels the trial in adult court. Although some states entitle juveniles to a jury trial, this is not a constitutional right (*McKeiver* v. *Pennsylvania*, 403 U.S. 528, 91 S. Ct. 1976 (1971)). At an adjudication hearing before a judge, the defense must argue for an acquittal and prosecutors must prove guilt "beyond a reasonable doubt" (*In re Winship*, 397 U.S. 358, 90 S. Ct. 1068 (1970)).

State studies of juvenile access to counsel (see sidebar on page 3) indicate that most juvenile cases—often as many as 90 percent—result in a plea bargain. Plea bargains are not inherently bad or even detrimental to the youth as long as they are not made for expediency's sake and the youth clearly is guilty. *Juvenile Justice Standards* (IJA-ABA, 1980) provides that a juvenile should not accept a plea bargain unless it is clear that the juvenile fully understands the alternative choices and the implications of a plea bargain in the event of rearrest or failure to adhere to sentencing and probation provisions. In the absence of effective counsel, however, juveniles may be unable to make an informed choice and may enter into a plea bargain because they do not fully understand the implications.

Disposition

At the disposition hearing, the court decides the placement, sanctions, and services the juvenile offender will receive. Dispositions may include (ranging from least to most restrictive) fines, community service, restitution, in-home probation, electronic monitoring, group home placement, and secure detention. Services may include psychological, psychiatric, and educational evaluation; individual and family counseling; substance abuse treatment; and medical care.

During the disposition hearing, legal counsel can help the judge identify the most appropriate sanctions and rehabilitative services for each juvenile. Counsel can present letters of support from teachers, churches, and community groups; educational and medical information; and other documents to aid the judge. However, if an attorney lacks the time and resources to investigate disposition options, a juvenile may be incarcerated even though a less expensive, more beneficial, and more appropriate alternative is available.

Postdisposition

Juvenile Justice Standards (IJA-ABA, 1980) indicates that legal representation for juveniles should not stop at disposition. Postdisposition activities include filing appeals, conducting periodic reviews of how the youth is faring, ensuring that the youth is receiving the services ordered and that placement remains appropriate, and addressing concerns for conditions of confinement.

In general, appeals are rare in juvenile court, possibly because sentences are short and the appeal process can be lengthy. Another contributing factor, as suggested by Puritz and colleagues (1995), may be that public defenders' offices are not organized to deal with appeals in juvenile cases. Subsequent state research by the ABA Juvenile Justice Center (see sidebar on page 3) has reported similar findings. When a felony offense is involved, however, an appeal may be in a juvenile's best interests because of the long-term ramifications of a felony conviction.

Factors That Hinder Access to and Quality of Juvenile Defense Counsel

A number of factors limit a juvenile's access to legal counsel and the quality of legal services provided. These factors may be broadly categorized as professional/procedural and policy-oriented/philosophical.

Professional/Procedural Factors

Professional/procedural factors include appointment of counsel, waiver of counsel, caseloads, compensation, use of motions, use of investigations, training, professional support, and organizational challenges. Each of these factors is discussed below.

Appointment of counsel. Access to legal counsel before and during the pretrial detention hearing is critical to the case. Yet state studies suggest that juveniles often do not have access to counsel at the early stages and that attorneys often lack sufficient leadtime to become familiar with their clients and the facts of the cases.

In Texas, researchers reported that no statewide or local systems exist for appointment of counsel; appointment is at the pleasure of individual judges, who have the power to determine compensation rates. Often, attorneys who bill at a lower rate are chosen. The first time that counsel must be present is at the adjudication hearing, not the detention hearing. Similarly, in Georgia, individual judges appoint counsel, sometimes from a list of attorneys under contract to the county. In Louisiana, some parents said that no attorney was appointed for their child, even when they had requested one, and some incarcerated youth said they had never met with an attorney or had spoken to one for less than 5 minutes prior to adjudication. In Kentucky, North Carolina, and Ohio, most attorneys who were surveyed reported that they are not appointed to represent youth until the detention hearing and often do not meet the youth until they are brought to court.

In several states, statutes require appointment of counsel at all stages of the proceedings. However, because there is no systemic mechanism to connect counsel and juvenile at the earliest point in the process, appointment often does not occur until a formal petition is filed in court.

Contrary to ABA Standards, Virginia law does not specifically provide for the right to counsel at arrest, intake, or the initial detention hearing. At intake, court services unit staff, rather than the prosecution, collect information about the youth; the defense counsel is prohibited from being present. Although the law prohibits statements made to the intake officer from being used against a youth at trial, it does not protect the youth from entering the system. Courts usually appoint counsel at the arraignment/initial detention hearing when youth are informed of the charges against them; however, counsel receives notice of the appointment *after* this hearing. Virginia is currently using video detention hearings, in which the youth remains at the detention center and addresses the court from that remote location. The youth has no court representation at that time and receives no explanation of the proceeding. Absence of counsel in the early stages of the process is a likely factor in Virginia's high rate of detention (nearly twice the national average) and in one of the biggest problems reported by juvenile defense attorneys: inadequate preparation and time with clients.

Maine's juvenile defenders are all appointed by the court from a list of private attorneys; there is no statewide, standardized system. Maine law requires that, during a youth's first appearance before the court (usually the detention hearing), youth and parents must be advised of the right to counsel at every step of the ensuing proceedings. However, juveniles do not have a statutory right to an attorney when arrested, although they cannot be denied access to a court-appointed attorney if they request one. Juvenile community corrections officers are authorized by Maine statute to conditionally release an arrested youth to parents, foster care, or an alternative facility. Detention must be in the least restrictive setting and cannot be ordered unless conditional release is inappropriate.

In Washington, children are generally represented by counsel at most juvenile proceedings; state law provides the right to counsel any time a threat of confinement exists. However, researchers found that representation varies significantly by county and that in some counties, the defender is never or rarely present at the "first appearance" hearing, which determines whether the youth should remain in detention until the next arraignment hearing.

Maryland and Pennsylvania have no uniform process to appoint public defenders and no eligibility criteria for indigency. In Maryland, indigent parents who need public defender services for a child face confusing procedures that vary from county to county. Parents may not have the required financial documentation or $25 intake fee to apply for services immediately or may not be aware that they must apply within a certain time period. In North Carolina, assessment of indigency is not uniformly applied. In addition, the state is inconsistent in its use of various mechanisms—even interception of state income tax refunds—to ensure collection of fees for defense services.

Waiver of counsel. *Juvenile Justice Standards* states that juveniles should be provided with counsel in all "delinquency or in need of supervision proceedings" (IJA-ABA, 1980, standard 2.3). *Gault* held that juveniles are entitled to counsel and that waiver can be made only by both the juvenile and a parent. In several states, statutes and case law prohibit or limit waiver of counsel by juveniles; those that permit waivers require proof that the youth understands the meaning and consequences of waiver, consider a waiver invalid unless it is informed by counsel, or grant waiver only after a juvenile consults with parents or guardians (Shepherd, 1998). Despite these protections, research indicates that too many juveniles are in effect denied right to counsel because they waive that right when clearly it is not in their best interests to do so.

In the ABA Juvenile Justice Center's 1995 national study (Puritz et al., 1995), 34 percent of public defenders' offices and a similar proportion of court-appointed counselors reported that some juveniles waive their rights at the detention hearing. Forty-six percent said that only "sometimes" or "rarely" is there an advisory colloquy with the judge before the youth waives this right. More recent interviews with state attorneys and court officers found that both the time the judges allot for colloquies and the quality of colloquies varied considerably. Reasons cited for waiver were that juveniles think their case is not very serious and parents fear the cost of engaging an attorney (perhaps unaware that one could be appointed free of charge or unable to navigate the eligibility procedures). In states with high waiver rates, researchers found that many juveniles waive counsel without ever talking to an attorney and do not understand what waiver means, and yet their competency to waive counsel is not challenged.

In Georgia, researchers found that delays in appointing counsel cause juveniles to be locked up for weekends, so some opt for waiver. Some counties require that parents apply for court-appointed counsel in person; if parents cannot take time away from work or do not fully understand the need for an attorney, they might decide to waive their child's right to counsel. Although parents in Georgia have the right to post bail if their child is arrested, some counties set bail at $2,500 or more, putting it out of reach for many low-income families. Georgia has no system for informing parents of their right to post bail and no bail-setting guidelines.

The Louisiana Children's Code states that juveniles have a right to counsel at every stage of the juvenile justice process. Nevertheless, some parishes reported that 80 to 90 percent of juveniles waive this right, and other parishes put the number at more than half. In 2 of 12 Ohio jurisdictions surveyed, waiver rates were as high as 80 percent. Virginia and Maryland reported waiver rates of about 50 percent. Pennsylvania reported a rate of 11 percent.

According to Montana statute, neither a youth nor parents may waive counsel if adjudication could result in a confinement of more than 6 months. However, when a youth is arrested or referred by a school to the juvenile justice system, a probation officer holds a "preliminary inquiry," and it is here that the youth could sign a waiver form. An attorney is not required at this inquiry because it is considered an informal hearing. Appointment of an attorney is not required until a petition is filed, usually 3 to 4 months later.

Kentucky's Court of Appeals has held that a youth can waive the right to counsel only if he or she is initially appointed counsel and the waiver is made intelligently, after consultation with counsel (*D.R. v. Commonwealth*, Ky. Ct. App., 64 S.W. 3d 292 (2001)). Two-thirds of attorneys who responded to Kentucky researchers reported that juveniles often or very often waive counsel at detention hearings, although nearly all juveniles who were incarcerated were represented by counsel. Ohio statute requires that waiver of counsel must be voluntary, knowing, and intelligent, but researchers found that many juveniles merely nod or say "ok" with little understanding. In Washington, youth may waive right to counsel, and it is up to the judge to ensure that they understand the consequences of that decision. According to defense attorneys in Washington, judges do not discuss the consequences or voluntary nature of waiver in approximately 70 percent of cases.

In Maine, waiver of counsel is not a problem. Many district judges spend time explaining the right to counsel to juveniles and their parents, and some judges refuse to accept waivers of counsel until a youth has spoken to an attorney.

Caseloads. During the last decade, the number of delinquency cases increased significantly. In 1999 (the latest year for which published statistics are available), the juvenile courts processed 1,673,000 cases, a 5-percent drop from the previous year, but a 27-percent increase from 1990 (Stahl, 2003). The number of defense attorneys and support personnel available to handle delinquency cases is not commensurate with the large volume of these cases. An overburdened attorney with insufficient time to become conversant with a case—particularly a complex case—is hard pressed to argue effectively for the client.

In its national survey, the ABA found that excessive caseloads were "the single most important barrier to effective representation" and led to burnout and job dissatisfaction (Puritz et al., 1995:8). Although the U.S. Bureau of Justice Assistance (2000) recommends an annual caseload no greater than 200 to 250 for public defenders handling juvenile cases on a full-time basis, national and state studies indicate that caseloads are much larger. The average juvenile caseload in the ABA's national survey was 300 (of a total caseload exceeding 500). Although not all states surveyed in 2000–2003 reported excessive caseload problems, the issue arose quite often, especially in urban jurisdictions. States reported annual delinquency caseloads as follows:

- Georgia: 200 to 350 for part-time defenders.
- Louisiana: as many as 800 per year.
- Kentucky: 500 to 1,000 (based on reports from two-thirds of Kentucky's jurisdictions). Note that the average caseload for a trial attorney in Kentucky was 421 in FY 2002, down 2 percent from FY 2000.
- Virginia: 679 to 1,500 for public defenders, 150 to 200 for court-appointed attorneys (representing 5 to 30 percent of their total caseload).
- Washington: 360 to 750.

Maryland and Pennsylvania do not collect data on caseload size. However, attorneys in these states reported numbers in excess of ABA Standards.

In many states surveyed, large caseloads result in an overdependence on probation officers, who often have more contact with youth—either in detention facilities or other placements—than do attorneys. Juveniles may not understand that the probation officer has no duty of confidentiality to them and that what they say to the officer can be used against them in court. When overburdened defense counsel rely on information from probation officers, the attorney's role as an advocate may be diluted.

Compensation. Indigent juveniles are represented either by public defenders who are salaried employees of state or local governments or by lawyers in private practice who are appointed from a panel by the courts. Research shows that compensation levels for attorneys who represent juveniles are inadequate in many jurisdictions and are generally not commensurate with compensation in other areas of legal practice. Many jurisdictions put caps on the number of hours a court-appointed attorney (i.e., not a public defender) can bill to a case or on overall spending per case. Examples of state compensation rates and fee structures follow.

- Georgia counties that comply with state supreme court guidelines pay court-appointed attorneys $60 per hour for in-court work and $45 per hour for out-of-court work; defenders who are under contract to counties do not receive benefits or reimbursement for overhead costs. Some Georgia counties cap the amount that attorneys can receive for each case; in one large urban county, the cap is $300. These compensation rates are well below market rates attorneys receive for nonappointed adult criminal cases. Furthermore, not all counties comply with the court's guidelines.
- In 2001, Kentucky raised starting salaries for entry-level public defenders in the Department of Public Advocacy from $23,388 to $35,000; starting salaries for experienced attorneys increased 9 percent.
- In Louisiana, compensation for public defenders and court-appointed defense attorneys representing juveniles ranges from $22,000 to $30,000 per year and often does not include

benefits. Some Louisiana jurisdictions severely limit payments for investigations and expert witnesses. Most of these defenders work only part-time on juvenile cases, supplementing their income by representing adults; those who work part-time must supply their own office space, telephone, computers, and supplies.

♦ Maine's juvenile defense attorneys are paid $50 per hour, but there is a cap of $315 per case.

♦ Pay for public defenders in Maryland is significantly lower than salaries for employees in comparable positions in other state agencies, according to a study by the state's Department of Budget and Management.

♦ In Montana, compensation rates for defense attorneys are set by county commissioners. In some counties, attorneys are paid a flat rate. Sometimes, office expenses are not reimbursed at all and travel is reimbursed minimally, at the state rate (a disincentive to travel the long distances often required to visit clients).

♦ Since 1986, attorneys in New York, NY, who are appointed to represent juveniles have received $40 per hour for in-court work and $25 per hour for out-of-court work (Fritsch and Rohde, 2001). New York rates were challenged in a lawsuit against the state and the city (*New York County Lawyers' Association* v. *State of New York and City of New York*, 763 N.Y.S.2d 397, decided February 5, 2003). In November 2003, the New York County Lawyers' Association settled with the state and city, which had appealed a state supreme court ruling that raised the rate to $90 per hour. Effective January 1, 2004, private counsel assigned to represent children and the poor in court proceedings in New York City receive $75 per hour for work on felony criminal cases and $60 per hour for work on misdemeanor cases.

♦ In the Ohio counties surveyed, starting salaries for full-time public defenders range from $35,000 to $42,000, and hourly rates for court-appointed counsel range from $40 to $60 for in-court work and $30 to $50 for out-of-court work.

♦ Salaries for public defenders in Pennsylvania are much lower than prosecutors' salaries. In Centre County, for example, the district attorney's salary is $116,000 and the chief public defender's is $57,000.

♦ In Texas, some defense attorneys are not compensated for out-of-court preparatory work, work on disposition issues, and postdisposition followup, and may be paid a flat rate per case or a set fee for the first court appearance and lower fees for each subsequent appearance.

♦ Legal representation in approximately half of all juvenile cases in Virginia is by court-appointed attorneys, whose compensation is limited to $110 per case. Plea bargaining is the norm in these cases.

Even though compensation for juvenile defense attorneys has improved somewhat in some jurisdictions, low compensation levels continue to affect recruitment and retention. First-year associates at firms of more than 250 attorneys earn on average $110,000, according to 2003 data compiled by the National Association for Law Placement (Luczycki, 2003). In 2002, the average debtload nationwide for graduating lawyers was more than $80,000 (Chase and Gonnell, 2003; Equal Justice Works, National Association for Law Placement, and Partnership for Public Service, 2002). In light of these facts, it is understandable that new attorneys may be reluctant to enter public service, even if they have a strong interest in juvenile defense work. The ABA national survey found that 55 percent of juvenile defense attorneys remained in their positions less than 2 years, and state surveys found that low compensation contributed to high staff turnover.

An additional concern is the potential effect of fee caps on the quality of defense. Because investigations, interviews, and testimony from expert witnesses (including medical, mental health, and other professionals) are essential in presenting evidence, fee caps and other limitations severely hamper an attorney's ability to mount an effective defense. Fee caps are also an incentive for less scrupulous attorneys to accept a large number of cases but stint on preparatory work.

Use of motions. Among the important elements of a zealous defense are pretrial motions and motions to suppress evidence on constitutional grounds. Only 30 percent of public defenders and court-appointed counsel surveyed by the ABA Juvenile Justice Center in 1995 said they filed pretrial motions. Of those who did file pretrial motions, many used "boilerplate" motions and standard form pleadings.

In general, use of motions is the exception rather than the rule in most states studied by the ABA between 2000 and 2003. Even when motions are made, they usually are oral and not supported by legal briefs. However, the quality and quantity of motions varies by state and county, depending on caseload size and courthouse culture. For example, since 1996, when Kentucky first surveyed its juvenile system, motion practice has improved. Today, nearly two-thirds of Kentucky public defender offices surveyed reported that they routinely file motions to suppress, motions for discovery (including depositions and interrogatories), motions regarding competency, and motions *in limine* (a pretrial request that certain inadmissible evidence not be referred to or offered at trial).

Use of investigations. Another element of an effective defense is the use of investigations. Thorough investigations may uncover witnesses and physical evidence that are helpful to the defense. The Georgia study found that juvenile defense attorneys rarely conduct investigations, possibly because hourly rates are lower for out-of-court work than in-court work, or because of dollar caps on cases. Rather than filing discovery motions, attorneys often rely on the prosecutor's discovery—a practice that necessitates a friendly relationship with opposing counsel. In North Carolina, 44 percent of attorneys surveyed reported that they rarely or never see the police report or other investigative material before their first meeting with the client, and 44 percent reported that they had no or inadequate access to investigators. This finding was echoed in other states, where attorneys reported that they did not have access to trained, experienced investigators (such as social workers and law clerks) and, because of large caseloads, could not conduct adequate investigations themselves.

Training. Training and mentoring are important ingredients for increasing the knowledge and skills of juvenile defense attorneys. Research indicates, however, that such training rarely takes place. Of the public defenders' offices surveyed in the 1995 ABA study, 78 percent said they had no budget for training juvenile defense attorneys; 50 percent did not have a training program for new attorneys, and 48 percent had no ongoing training program; 46 percent lacked a training manual for juvenile defense practice; and 32 percent had no training manual at all. Offices that did have training programs often omitted important topics, such as pretrial motions, alternatives to detention, and child development.

The following summaries are based on state reports to ABA researchers between 2000 and 2003.

♦ Georgia has no training standards for juvenile defense attorneys and no funding for training and continuing education. Most attorneys surveyed said they see no need for training because they "learn on the job."

♦ Kentucky's Department of Public Advocacy conducted a training needs assessment that resulted in some improvements. Co-counseling (pairing a new attorney with an experienced attorney) has proven to be an effective training tool. New attorneys also hold case reviews with other juvenile defense attorneys, including an experienced trial attorney and a postdisposition attorney for complex cases. The Department of Public Advocacy conducts regular regional workshops and uses the Internet and e-mail listservs to keep juvenile defense attorneys up to date on practice issues.

♦ The Louisiana Public Defenders Association offers a 2-day training program for juvenile defense attorneys; however, unlike prosecutors, defenders are not compensated for attending continuing education classes.

♦ Maine has no training requirement and scant access to continuing education for juvenile defense attorneys. Until 2002, these attorneys had to travel out of state for continuing education. Those in rural areas still must drive 8 to 10 hours to attend classes.

♦ Maryland's Office of the Public Defender offers juvenile defense attorneys a 1-week training program twice a year, with two followup sessions. Although Maryland requires attorneys to complete 12 hours of continuing education per year, specific training in juvenile defense is not mandatory. In FY 2002, only 19 attorneys attended classes in juvenile defense.

♦ In Montana, opportunities for training in juvenile defense are minimal, and most defense attorneys do not specialize in juvenile cases.

♦ North Carolina respondents noted that in addition to more training in juvenile law and procedure, they saw a need for other training specific to representing juveniles, including interviewing techniques, conflict resolution, verbal de-escalation skills, and counseling. Law schools at the University of North Carolina and North Carolina Central University operate clinics where law students represent youth in delinquency proceedings. The Children's Education Law Clinic at Duke University School of Law engages in special education advocacy. Clinics at law schools offer students valuable opportunities to work under supervision in special practice areas such as juvenile defense.

♦ In Ohio, lack of training and inexperience of defenders were apparent to researchers from their observations of court proceedings and interviews of incarcerated youth.

♦ In Pennsylvania, several judges said they resented the responsibility of ensuring that new attorneys adequately represent their clients.

♦ In Texas, juvenile defense appointments are used as a training ground for adult criminal court, and no jurisdiction has either a training program or a formal mentoring program for inexperienced attorneys.

♦ The Virginia code does not require juvenile defense attorneys to have training or experience. The one annual juvenile court training session is not mandatory. Court-appointed counsel must pay for their own training. For public defenders, the Commonwealth subsidizes training to meet requirements of the bar, but defenders must pay for any additional training themselves.

♦ In Washington, training availability for juvenile defense attorneys is excellent in King County (Seattle) but drops off markedly in other counties.

Professional support. To function effectively, juvenile defense attorneys need certain basic elements of professional support, including online legal research capability, paralegals, bilingual staff, and adequate space for interviews. Professional support also includes access to and funds to hire expert witnesses, such as psychiatrists, social workers, and forensic specialists. The ABA's 1995 national study found that these elements often were lacking.

Forty-six percent of respondents in the 1995 survey did not have access to specialized texts, 64 percent did not have access to online Westlaw or Lexis legal databases, and 56 percent had no paralegal support. Even in 2002, only approximately 50 percent of attorneys who responded to the ABA survey in Ohio reported that they had access to Westlaw, Lexis, or other online research services. Lack of meeting space for private interviews with clients was cited as a problem in Texas; New Orleans Parish, LA; Montana; North Carolina; and some Ohio counties.

Among offices that often serve non-English-speaking clients, 83 percent lacked bilingual staff and 43 percent did not have translators available in 1995. In Texas, where most court-appointed attorneys were solo practitioners with no staff support, lack of translation services was also a problem. North Carolina reported a lack of cultural competence among juvenile defense attorneys concerning new immigrants to the state, primarily Spanish-speaking, Vietnamese, and Hmong groups. Pennsylvania respondents noted that the number of Latino clients was increasing but the number of certified Spanish-language interpreters was not. Often, Latino defendants in Pennsylvania had to translate court proceedings for their parents.

In Ohio, approximately two-thirds of those responding to the ABA survey reported inadequate access to mental health professionals, one-third lacked adequate paralegal assistance, and less than half had adequate investigation assistance. Attorneys in Virginia, Maryland, Montana, North Carolina, and Pennsylvania reported a similar lack of support staff, law clerks, investigators, and experts (mental health, education, etc.). In Virginia, however, some jurisdictions reported hiring sentencing advocates who investigate mitigating evidence to present to the court in sentencing hearings, although these advocates focus primarily on adult cases. In rural counties of Montana and Maryland, breaches of confidentiality, long distances between facilities, and lack of collateral support services were reported as problems.

Organizational challenges. Professional support also includes an organizational culture in which aggressive defense of juveniles is valued rather than regarded as an impediment to efficiency. In the ABA study, one interviewee said that "to maintain a 'friendly' atmosphere in the courthouse is more important than 'looking like a genius'" (Puritz et al., 1995:51). In the Texas study, several attorneys reported that they were pressured to elicit guilty pleas and were removed from appointment lists if they were considered to be "too aggressive" or even if they refused to contribute to a judge's reelection campaign. The situation in Washington—a team-spirited, friendly philosophy that applauds congeniality among probation, prosecution, defense, and judges—is less contentious but still troubling in its implications for juvenile defendants (see discussion of due process in the next section). In Montana, the courtroom philosophy is more punitive: some judges, prosecutors, and probation officers viewed zealous advocacy negatively as a means to "getting the kid off."

In North Carolina, several court-appointed attorneys said they believed that juveniles and their parents caused the problems. These attorneys, who cited juveniles' lack of discipline and refusal to take responsibility for their behavior, apparently assumed their clients were guilty. Although North Carolina's Juvenile Code holds parents liable for contempt for failure to comply in their child's disposition orders, the court does not help parents comply (e.g., by allowing flexible court hours so that working parents can meet with personnel, informing parents of the importance of involvement, or assisting with transportation).

Researchers in Virginia described the culture in juvenile courts as unprofessional, rude, and humiliating to families. In some courts, probation officers—not Commonwealth's attorneys—prosecuted juvenile cases. Probation officers stood next to defenders, so that defenders could not speak confidentially to their clients. Juvenile court hearings are not recorded, and there is no transcript of record. Juvenile defense is not viewed as a respectable profession in Virginia. Court-appointed lawyers refuse to take juvenile cases, and public defenders move to adult court when they gain experience.

Policy Factors and Philosophical Issues

Other factors affecting legal representation for juveniles relate to changes in state policies that govern sanctions for juvenile offenders and to basic due process issues that arise as courts seek both to rehabilitate juveniles and to protect the community.

State policies. In light of recent state policies that encourage tougher sanctions for juvenile offenders, it is especially important for all juveniles to be represented by competent attorneys who provide a zealous defense. These policies are a response, in part, to dramatic media reports about juvenile crime and to the public's perception that such crime has become more prevalent and more severe (Dorfman and Schiraldi, 2001).

In considering the implications of state policies that encourage tougher sanctions for juvenile offenders, it is important to keep in mind that racial minorities and youth with educational, mental health, and substance abuse problems are overrepresented in juvenile courts (Hawkins et al., 2000). A consensus from state and national studies indicates that there is a paucity of services to meet the needs of these youth. A defense attorney who can navigate the interrelated educational, health, and social services systems to find appropriate services for these clients (i.e., culturally relevant services for minority youth and services that address special needs) is better able to mount an effective argument against pretrial detention, incarceration, or waiver to adult court and in favor of diversion to rehabilitative programs.

Due process. The rules of professional conduct, a version of which exists in each state, provide that "a lawyer shall abide by a client's decisions concerning the objectives of representation . . ." (*ABA Model Rules of Professional Conduct*, Rule 1.2, ABA, 2002). Under most states' rules of professional conduct, the attorney must promote the child's wishes because the child is the client; the attorney must not make personal judgments about what is in the child's best interests. Nevertheless, researchers in Georgia heard a "best interests of the child" argument for not aggressively pursuing a juvenile's defense. A juvenile court judge in that state "described the approach of the juvenile court as a 'conspiracy of justice' where a 'huge bond of trust' exists that ensures a non-adversarial environment with everyone believing they are acting in the best interests of the child" (Puritz and Sun, 2001:31). In Ohio, researchers found the "best interest" role so pervasive that there was no perceived value in having an attorney represent the youth. In Maine, one judge said: "A good juvenile defender is: committed to kids, has a passion for justice for kids . . . they try to work for best interest of the kids and create a solution that will avoid the return of the kid to court."

With this kind of approach, however, defense counsel faces a conflict between vigorously defending the client and acting in more of a social worker's capacity to promote the child's best interests as well as to ensure harmonious relations with the court. In Maryland, respondents in some counties reported that the standard of guilt was changed from "beyond a reasonable doubt" in favor of a child's "best interests," resulting in adjudication without due process of law. In Washington, defense attorneys expressed confusion, ambivalence, and disagreement over their dual role as an advocate for both due process and rehabilitation services—a "false dichotomy," according to researchers. The Washington researchers pointed out that a defense attorney can work to ensure that the due process rights of the client are not violated while at the same time trying to secure services for the youth (e.g., an attorney can argue that a youth be diverted to a substance abuse program or perform community service rather than be adjudicated).

Elements Necessary for Quality Counsel

The Sentencing Project outlined a series of elements that are critical to effective juvenile defense (Young and Gainsborough, 2000). Although the Sentencing Project report focuses primarily on youth prosecuted as adults, these elements are germane to the defense of juveniles in both juvenile and criminal court. The elements, discussed below, include valid assessment; knowledge of youth development; access to experts, information, and community resources; building on family strengths; appropriate defense strategies; and integration of juvenile defense with other systems.

Valid Assessment

Public defender programs should have appropriate, validated instruments and skilled staff to ascertain the needs of youth who have been arrested and assess the risk they may pose to the community. The instruments should provide an accurate account of each youth's mental health status, use of alcohol and illegal substances, educational level, family background, history of abuse and/or neglect, flight risk, and threat to the community. Programs should have adequate funds and staff to handle this task.

Knowledge of Youth Development

Attorneys who represent juveniles should understand that it takes time and effort to build rapport with a youth who may mistrust any adult, no matter how helpful that adult is trying to be. Juvenile defense attorneys should be familiar with the risk and protective factors that influence youth behavior and should know about youth culture, gangs, peer pressure, and use of alcohol and illegal drugs.[4] Attorneys should understand cognitive and emotional development (National Council of Juvenile and Family Court Judges, 2001). They should be aware that negative, critical, or condescending attitudes or comments on the part of court personnel might psychologically damage juveniles and should also take care that clients do not hear diagnoses they would not understand and might misconstrue. Attorneys should also realize that youth and adults have different concepts of time. A youth's perspective is more immediate, and his or her attention span is shorter. Therefore, a youth may interpret delays between hearings as an indication that a situation is not serious.

Research conducted by the MacArthur Foundation confirms what most who work with youth suspect: "Children and adolescents do not and cannot think like adults. They are neither emotionally or cognitively mature enough to understand the full ramifications of their actions or what will transpire once they enter the legal system." However, the need for child development training and guidance for juvenile justice personnel has been largely ignored (Steinberg, 2003:21).

Access to Experts, Information, and Community Resources

Attorneys representing juvenile clients should have access to social workers, child psychologists, educators, substance abuse treatment professionals, and other experts who can help them with youth development issues. These experts should be part of the defense team. Information about treatment, education, social services, and alternatives to incarceration should be readily available to defense attorneys, so they will be aware of these resources for their clients and be in a position to recommend options to judges.

---

[4]Many publications on delinquency risk and protective factors are available from OJJDP. Visit the publications section of the OJJDP Web site at www.ojp.usdoj.gov/ojjdp.

Attorneys should also know of gaps in services, as it is pointless to recommend, for example, drug treatment for a client if no services are available. Furthermore, the Sentencing Project recommends that attorneys continue their advocacy after clients are referred for services, to ensure that providers do not fail the youth sent to them.

Building on Family Strengths

To mount an effective defense, counsel should communicate with the juvenile's family (biological parents, adoptive parents, relatives, or other guardians). Family members can provide background information about the youth and, possibly, information about the alleged offense. Defense attorneys should have the necessary resources to conduct family investigations, which can be time consuming and costly.

Appropriate Defense Strategies

Juvenile defense attorneys need to be aware that certain defenses may be posed for juveniles that would not be used for adults. These defenses include infancy, incompetency, lack of criminal intent, and lack of culpability. Infancy and incompetency refer not to impairment but rather to a youth's age or level of psychological development (infancy applies to minor children; incompetency is the lack of legal ability to stand trial or testify). Incapacity is the lack of physical or mental capabilities to have certain legal consequences attach to an action (e.g., a child has an incapacity to make a binding contract). Lack of culpability refers to the absence of evidence that a person acted purposely, knowingly, recklessly, or negligently (Black and Garner, 2000).

Integration of Juvenile Defense With Other Systems

Improving access to legal counsel within the juvenile justice system requires broad-based change that encompasses how attorneys relate to their clients and to each other, their knowledge concerning children and youth, and their interactions with other systems (e.g., social services, health care, education). Efforts to improve access to legal counsel for juveniles can and should be integrated with other systems. Results from state surveys reveal factors affecting such integration (see sidebar on page 17).

Although traditionally associated with delinquency proceedings for youth who have been arrested, legal counsel for juveniles is also appropriate for other types of court proceedings such as status offenses, abuse and neglect hearings, special education advocacy, domestic violence, and landlord-tenant disputes. Interrelated issues often underlie these proceedings. For example, a status offense may lead to a delinquency hearing if the youth violates a court order, child abuse may be a factor in chronic truancy or running away from home, and inability to obtain affordable housing may create overwhelming family stress that can lead to contacts with the legal system. Such underlying issues may not surface or receive sufficient consideration in juvenile court. Attorneys who can bring their knowledge of the law to bear on these issues may be able to intervene on behalf of a youth early enough to initiate appropriate individual and family services that can prevent further penetration into the juvenile justice system.

Factors Affecting Integration of Juvenile Defense With Other Systems: State Survey Findings

School systems. Survey respondents in Kentucky, Maine, Maryland, North Carolina, Ohio, and Virginia reported that schools were too often relying on the courts to handle issues of safety and potential violence. Zero tolerance policies and criminalization of what is merely bad behavior in the classroom can land a child in juvenile court and even prison. In Kentucky, respondents reported concern that schools were inappropriately releasing confidential information to the courts, whereas Maryland respondents reported difficulty accessing school records. In 2002, North Carolina established a Special Education Juvenile Justice Project in five pilot counties through a grant from the Governor's office. The objectives of the project are to provide direct special education advocacy, offer training about special education rights of juveniles with disabilities, provide technical assistance, and promote referrals and evaluations of juveniles with special education needs.

Mental health. In all states surveyed by the ABA teams, respondents reported that youth with mental health problems were greatly overrepresented in the juvenile justice system and also reported a severe shortage of treatment resources for these youth, particularly in rural areas. In many states, respondents characterized the juvenile justice system as the dumping ground for youth with severe mental health problems and said the system is unequipped to meet the needs of these youth.

American Indian populations. In states with large American Indian populations, juvenile defense attorneys experience unique difficulties in working with multiple agencies and jurisdictions: the federal government's Bureau of Indian Affairs and Indian Health Service, tribal governments, and state and county governments.

How States Are Addressing Issues

Some states have improved access to and the quality of counsel for indigent juveniles through systems change efforts. Approaches, discussed in the following sections, include (1) special program initiatives funded by federal, state, and local governments or private organizations; (2) new legislation that requires a change in current practices; (3) administrative reforms that introduce new policies and procedures; (4) research to inform program development; and (5) litigation to redress violation of an individual youth's rights or the rights of a class of youth.

Special Program Initiatives

California. The Annie E. Casey Foundation sponsored the Juvenile Detention Alternatives Initiative in Sacramento, CA, and four other U.S. communities in 1993. In Sacramento, the initiative addressed a dysfunctional and overcrowded juvenile court system through the formation of a public sector partnership between county prosecutors and defense attorneys. Both parties agreed to an "early resolution" process by which youth eligible for community-based alternatives to detention could avoid trial. The benefit to the defense was complete and open discovery provided very early in the case. The benefit to prosecutors was early settlement, freeing them to concentrate on more serious cases (Stanfield, 1999).

Colorado. To promote public awareness of juveniles' legal rights and improve legal advocacy for juveniles, Colorado is funding an information/training enhancement to the Web site of the new Office of the Child's Representative. The state also funded annual juvenile law conferences to enhance attorneys' knowledge and skills with regard to delinquency cases (Patricia Cervera, Colorado Juvenile Justice Specialist, personal communication, August 16, 2001).

Washington. In Washington, FY 2000 OJJDP funds were used to develop an interdisciplinary approach to legal representation for juveniles. The state established agreements with the Seattle University School of Law and School of Education to create a clinical law program that used psychologists and special education experts to train juvenile defense attorneys and law students. The program trained 85 attorneys, including 45 in private practice who agreed to participate in a new pro bono panel to represent juveniles. In cooperation with the TeamChild project (see page 26), the university developed a special education manual, a curriculum, and a juvenile resource manual and also provided consultation services in juvenile delinquency cases. An evaluation found that the program's consultation services made a significant difference in the level and quality of representation provided to juveniles.

New Legislation

Illinois. In 2000, Illinois enacted legislation (Public Act 91–0577) establishing a task force to study caseloads, salary structures, technological needs, and other issues affecting recruitment and retention of public defenders and assistant prosecutors in the state's justice system. In January 2001, the first state law requiring early access to counsel for children in police custody went into effect in Illinois (Public Act 91–0915). The law requires counsel to be present at the station house during interrogation of juveniles younger than 13 who are suspects in murder or sexual assault cases.

Washington. Washington is the only state with mandatory sentencing guidelines for juveniles. Under the state's Juvenile Justice Act, certain minor offenses require diversion of juveniles to perform community service, make restitution to the victim, attend counseling, and possibly pay a fine of up to $100. Although the diversion program is considered a model, cases referred to diversion between 1991 and 2001 decreased 21 percent while charges filed increased 19 percent during the same period. In July 2003, a new law went into effect that allows various disposition alternatives, including suspended disposition on the condition that the offender complies with local sanctions and treatment programs, a chemical dependency alternative requiring treatment instead of incarceration, and a mental health alternative that allows the court to order a comprehensive mental health evaluation and psychiatric treatment. A fourth alternative, known as "manifest injustice," allows judges to deviate upward or downward from the sentencing guidelines based on mitigating and aggravating factors. Judges may take into account factors such as the parent's involvement and effectiveness and the youth's school status and participation in treatment.

Administrative Reforms

Illinois. In Illinois, OJJDP grant funding was used to assess the quality of counsel for juveniles and to improve juvenile defense as part of a statewide effort to reduce disproportionate minority confinement (Clark, 2001). In a policy reform that is likely to have positive administrative consequences within the juvenile justice system, the Illinois Juvenile Justice Commission and Department of Human Services together endorsed the Charter for Illinois Children. The charter, which is the product of a statewide collaboration of child advocacy groups, social services agencies, and community organizations, seeks to promote the well-being of children through public policy and has among its goals equal protection and due process of law for all youth (Illinois Department of Human Services, 2000).

In Cook County, the Public Defender's Office Detention Response Unit, in an effort to improve procedure, began interviewing detained juveniles and their families prior to the first court appearance. Between December 1997 and May 1998, 49 percent of youth interviewed were released from detention because alternative plans were submitted to the court. This success led to the addition of two paralegal positions to expand the Detention Response Unit project (Henry, 1999).

Oregon. During the mid-1990s, the Multnomah County Metropolitan Defenders Service began taking social histories of juvenile clients early in the court process rather than waiting until adjudication. (Social histories facilitate the discovery process and provide background information that might be relevant at a hearing.) This change meant that defenders were better prepared to discuss appropriate placements and could speed up the disposition process (Henry, 1999).

Research To Inform Program Development

Colorado. In FY 2000, Colorado targeted disproportionate minority confinement (DMC) as an inherent problem associated with lack of representation and/or lack of adequate representation (Colorado Department of Public Safety, 2000). After completing Phases I and II of OJJDP's DMC requirement, Colorado formed the Coalition for Minority Youth, which joined with the Access to Counsel Advisory Board to study several communities, including Mesa County (see description of Mesa County Partners, under "Promising Programs," page 21). The coalition uses data and research findings to effect change through special program initiatives.

Missouri. In 1998, the University of Missouri-St. Louis was awarded OJJDP funds to study the issue of legal representation in cases involving serious delinquency charges. Examining cases in urban, suburban, and rural counties, researchers found that legal counsel represented only 32 percent of 469 juveniles charged with felonies. Surprisingly, a disposition of out-of-home placement was more likely if a youth had an attorney (Burruss and Kempf-Leonard, 2000). The study's final report was shared with juvenile judges and juvenile officers in all of Missouri's 45 circuits.

Litigation To Redress Violations of Rights

Litigation, though costly and contentious, can serve to force the justice system to better safeguard the rights of juveniles by recruiting, training, and improving working conditions of juvenile defense attorneys. Claiming that excessively high caseloads and inadequate resources resulted in poor representation for indigent clients, the Connecticut Civil Liberties Union brought suit on behalf of public defenders against the Governor for violations of the 6th and 14th amendments (*Rivera* v. *Rowland*, Conn. Super. Ct., CV–95–0545629 (1996), cited in Cooper, Puritz, and Shang, 1998). The Supreme Court of Louisiana found that working conditions for public defenders in New Orleans Parish resulted in lack of effective counsel (*State* v. *Peart*, 621 So. 2d 780 (1993), cited in Cooper, Puritz, and Shang, 1998). As a result of this finding, more public defenders were hired; however, the study of juvenile defense in Louisiana suggests that serious deficiencies still exist (Celeste, 2001).

As mentioned earlier, New York's low compensation rates for juvenile defense attorneys and attorneys representing the poor were challenged in a lawsuit, triggered in part by a 2001 series in the *New York Times* about conditions for and insufficient numbers of public defenders (*New York County Lawyers' Association* v. *State of New York and City of New York*, 763 N.Y.S.2d 397, decided February 5, 2003). In a particularly interesting case, Quitman County in Mississippi sued the state, claiming that the state breached its duty to provide adequate representation for indigent criminal defendants. The Supreme Court of Mississippi affirmed that the county could bring a constitutional challenge against the state. At the time this Bulletin was written, the case was on remand for a full trial on the merits (*State of Mississippi* v. *Quitman County*, 807 So. 2d 401 (Miss. 2001)).

Promising Programs

Among the five approaches discussed above, the most frequently adopted is the development of special program initiatives to enhance access to effective juvenile counsel. A number of programs include elements considered necessary for effectively defending juvenile clients, such as valid assessments, knowledge of youth development, access to information and experts, emphasis on risk and protective factors, access to community resources, culturally relevant services for minority youth, and services that address special needs. Some of these programs have also demonstrated positive changes in access to and quality of counsel.

This section does not attempt to present an exhaustive list of programs but rather describes six programs that illustrate a range of promising initiatives that state and local agencies have undertaken to address issues that affect access to counsel. Some of the programs use federal OJJDP funds allocated by their states. Others are supported by state money appropriated through the legislatures. Still others receive funding from foundations and private sources. Most rely on a combination of funding sources.

First Defense Legal Aid

Since its formation in 1994, First Defense Legal Aid (FDLA) has provided legal aid to adult and juvenile residents of Chicago, IL. During this period, legal representation for Chicago minors has increased from 11 percent annually to 22 percent. In Illinois (and many other states), police can question a suspect for up to 72 hours without the presence of legal counsel. Public defenders cannot be appointed until a defendant appears in court and indigence is determined. FDLA bridges this gap in legal representation, intervening at the outset of all cases involving juveniles. This early intervention is especially important for juveniles, who, because of their youth and inexperience with the legal system, can easily be intimidated into making false statements.

FDLA attorneys respond to an average of 25 to 50 calls per day, 700 to 1,500 calls per month. They provide consultation over the phone. They also go to the police station if an individual is being subjected to custodial interrogation, as youth often do not understand their rights and may unwittingly make statements against their interests as a result of coercion, intimidation, or confusion. FDLA attorneys also ensure that clients' special needs (such as receiving medical attention or prescribed medications while in police custody) are being met. In addition, they document and report any violations of procedural or legal rights that may occur while clients are in police custody.

FDLA offers legal advice and educates the public about the criminal and juvenile justice systems. It conducts outreach through street law programs,[5] public service announcements, social workers, and various agencies. With the addition of an education coordinator to the staff, FDLA expanded its education and outreach capabilities considerably. During the first half of 2001, FDLA made 190 public education presentations at area high schools, elementary schools, social services agencies, halfway houses, and churches. By providing peer educator training in more than half of Chicago's public schools, FDLA has been able to increase the juvenile population it serves.

FDLA emphasizes its "train the trainers" initiative, which identifies community leaders and shows them how to present FDLA's public education program. In this way, basic "know your rights" information is communicated regularly to staff and clientele of a variety of educational and social services agencies. The FDLA staff also conducts training on specific legal issues such as search and seizure, "criminalization" of youth, and juvenile rights.

In September 2000, FDLA opened an office in Chicago's Englewood community. A National Association for Public Interest Law staff attorney assigned to the Englewood office provides early-intervention legal representation and public education to community residents. FDLA's Project E.A.G.L.E. (Englewood Access to Genuine Legal Empowerment) was undertaken in response to a growing rift between Englewood residents and Chicago police. Englewood was in the national news in 1999 when detectives claimed that two children, ages 7 and 8, confessed to the murder of an 11-year-old. DNA evidence later exonerated the children, bringing public attention to the failure of police

---

[5]Street law programs, which started in 1972 as a Georgetown University Law School project and were replicated across the country, provide youth with practical knowledge about the law.

to properly investigate crimes in this neighborhood. The way the police handled the homicide investigation accentuated the need for guaranteed free legal representation and legal education in Chicago's poor communities.

FDLA's role expanded further in 2001 with the passage of Illinois Public Act 91–0915. This law requires early access to legal counsel for children younger than 13 who are in police custody and who have been accused of homicide or sexual assault.

FDLA receives no government funding. Its funding sources include the United Way, Field Foundation, Chicago Community Trust, Public Welfare Foundation, Illinois Bar Foundation, Chicago Bar Foundation, Louis Lurie Foundation, Woods Fund of Chicago, Open Society Institute, National Association for Public Interest Law, and WPWR-Channel 50 Foundation.

For additional information on FDLA, contact:

Darron Bowden, Esq.
Director
First Defense Legal Aid
3645 West Chicago Avenue, Suite 240
Chicago, IL 60651
773–826–6550
773–722–4997 (fax)
frstdefens@aol.com

Mesa County Partners

Mesa County Partners in Grand Junction, CO, has shown considerable promise in tackling overrepresentation of minorities in the juvenile justice system. Mesa County's chief judge was aware of the county's DMC problem as early as 1993, when court data revealed that minority (predominantly Hispanic) youth constituted 60 percent of all youth in the juvenile justice system, compared with 12 percent in the general population. Analysis of the data found little difference between minority and nonminority youth with regard to seriousness of crimes committed or number of police contacts. The overrepresentation of minorities emerged at the commitment stage because minority juveniles often did not have an attorney, did not understand or trust the system, and had not appeared in court for previous offenses (with the result that these offenses, which usually were minor, accumulated until the judge ordered incarceration).

Mesa County Partners formed its Minority Family Advocacy Project in 1995 to work with minority youth who become involved with the juvenile justice system. The program uses 2 staff advocates and 12 bilingual volunteer family advocates who walk juveniles through the system, help them obtain defense counsel, and make sure the juveniles know their rights. The staff advocates attend all detention hearings, see that paperwork reaches the public defender or court-appointed attorney, and help youth understand the status of their case—work that public defenders often do not have time to do. The staff advocates, who work with approximately 100 youth at any given time, pair with 40 volunteer advocates, who spend 3 to 4 hours per week with the juveniles, as mentors, tutors, and friends. The program is funded with OJJDP Formula Grant funds through the Colorado Division of Criminal Justice and matching county funds. Stipends for the volunteers come from WRAP, an agency supported by the county's Division of Human Services and the local school system.

For additional information on Mesa County Partners, contact:

Joe Higgins
Executive Director
Mesa County Partners
735 South Avenue
Grand Junction, CO 81501
970–245–5555, ext. 18
970–245–7411 (fax)
partners@gi.net

New York Legal Aid Society

Founded in 1876, the New York Legal Aid Society in New York City is the nation's oldest and largest legal services organization (New York Legal Aid Society, 2000). The society has two components that deal with legal counsel for juveniles: the Juvenile Rights Division (JRD) and the Criminal Defense Division (CDD).

Juvenile Rights Division. JRD represents 90 percent of the youth who appear before the Family Court in New York City in cases involving abuse and neglect, delinquency, and persons-in-need-of-supervision status offenses. The division represented more than 36,000 youth in 2002; child protection cases far outnumbered delinquency cases.

JRD's delinquency teams represent children younger than 16 who are charged as delinquents in family court. Initiated a few years ago, delinquency teams now operate in four New York City boroughs: the Bronx, Brooklyn, Manhattan, and Queens. Teams consist of a supervising attorney and staff attorneys, a social worker, and an educational consultant from PEAK (Providing Educational Assistance to Kids), a JRD project that addresses education-related issues of delinquency clients. The teams also have access to paralegals, investigators, and interns. Social workers and PEAK educational specialists become involved in cases early in the process so they can prepare a dispositional plan and testify for an alternative to incarceration. If a youth is involved in both a child protection matter and a delinquency matter, a special team is created to coordinate the youth's representation. Team attorneys and educational consultants represent youth in any school suspension or other school-related proceeding. Team members meet regularly to discuss cases and strategies. JRD also has a delinquency practice group consisting of representatives from the four boroughs who meet to discuss citywide trends and legal issues. This group and the individual delinquency teams identify issues, such as conditions of confinement, to be addressed by JRD's special litigation unit.

JRD maintains a shared online directory, which includes a practice manual, recent case law, and a motions bank. The division also conducts ongoing training for unit staff, including specialized instruction for child protective services and delinquency matters. These specialized resources, together with the opportunity to focus exclusively on delinquency cases, enable team attorneys to gain greater expertise in legal and dispositional issues relevant to delinquency matters.

For additional information on JRD, contact:

Jacqueline Deane
Juvenile Rights Division
New York Legal Aid Society
304 Park Avenue South, Sixth Floor
New York, NY 10010
212–420–6200
646–654–7080 (fax)
jdeane@legal-aid.org

Criminal Defense Division. CDD represents juveniles charged as adults (youth ages 13–15 who are charged with serious felony offenses and youth 16 and older, who are considered adults under New York law). In 1996, CDD created a juvenile offender team in its Manhattan trial office to represent youth ages 13–15 who were charged in adult criminal court with violent felony offenses. These cases, which are prosecuted under New York's juvenile offender law, constitute a small percentage of CDD's total caseload yet require a great deal of time and attention. CDD formed a specialized team to handle juvenile offender cases because it recognized that effective legal representation for these youth requires specific expertise in child and adolescent development, psychiatric diagnoses prevalent among youth, and the effects of child abuse and neglect—areas not ordinarily familiar to attorneys trained to represent adults.

The multidisciplinary juvenile offender team consists of a director, seven experienced attorneys, an investigator, a forensic social worker, and a therapeutic social worker. The team meets biweekly to confer on cases, discuss case strategy, and share experiences from the courtroom and program referrals. Team members also share their specialized knowledge in case consultations with CDD attorneys and social workers who represent older teenagers.

CDD's team model emphasizes early case analysis to explore trial and sentencing strategies. Team members collect social, education, and mental health histories to enhance case advocacy. This approach results in speedier dispositions, fewer and shorter incarcerations, and greater use of alternatives to incarceration. In the majority of cases, the team secures placements in community-based programs that offer alternatives to incarceration. The team's therapeutic social worker, whose position is funded by grants from the Van Ameringen Foundation and the Bulova Fund, works onsite at a community-based program and in clients' homes, providing counseling and services to clients and their families. The therapeutic social worker intervenes in family crises and focuses on improving family members' communication and self-esteem.

CDD's juvenile offender team also works with special litigation units in CDD and JRD and with the Legal Aid Society's prisoner rights project to address, through litigation and legislation, issues facing incarcerated youth. The team also collaborates with JRD attorneys and social workers to coordinate advocacy for clients appearing in both family court and criminal court. Additionally, CDD juvenile offender team attorneys represent clients in school suspension and school placement matters. The team has also formed working relationships with education advocacy and youth services groups in the community and overall has significantly improved the level of advocacy provided to young people in New York City's adult criminal system.

For additional information on CDD, contact:

Nancy Ginsburg
Juvenile Offender Team
Criminal Defense Division
New York Legal Aid Society
49 Thomas Street
New York, NY 10013
212–298–5000
212–587–3179 (fax)
nginsburg@legal-aid.org

Public Defender Service for the District of Columbia

The Public Defender Service (PDS) for the District of Columbia was created in 1960. In 1970, the organization expanded and assumed its current name. The mission of PDS is to provide and promote quality legal representation for indigent adults and children who become involved in court proceedings in the District. PDS seeks to protect society's interest in the fair administration of justice. Although a major portion of the agency's work is devoted to ensuring that no innocent person is wrongfully convicted of a crime, PDS also provides legal representation for individuals who are facing involuntary civil commitment in the mental health system and for children in the delinquency system who have disabilities. The strength of PDS has always been the quality of the legal services it delivers. PDS concentrates its resources on complex and serious cases and has developed considerable institutional knowledge and expertise that it leverages to the legal community through training and consultation.

Since its creation in 2002, the Family Court of the Superior Court of the District of Columbia has had jurisdiction over children who are charged with delinquent acts, as well as all proceedings involving neglect, divorce, custody, adoption, and other family-related matters. Under the "one family, one judge" requirement of the Family Court, the same judge is assigned to all such matters involving the same child whenever it is practical, feasible, and lawful to do so. This system provides continuity for juvenile public defenders. The Family Court judges become more familiar with the cases, and the defenders are likely to have better access to guardians ad litem, education advocates, social workers, and others assigned to a case. In general, the system is intended to provide a more teamlike, family-oriented approach to child welfare and juvenile justice.

PDS has incorporated many effective elements in its juvenile defense activities on behalf of individual clients and brings about system change largely by training non-PDS lawyers who represent juvenile clients. PDS has developed a specialty curriculum on juvenile defense and periodically conducts comprehensive training for attorneys who practice in delinquency court. PDS also offers training sessions and conferences on special education advocacy and disability law as they relate to juveniles in the delinquency system. For example, in 2002, PDS conducted a training series on Hot Topics in Education and Community-Based Services for Children With Disabilities in the Juvenile Justice System. Participants in these training events include defense and special education attorneys who practice in the delinquency and neglect courts, as well as civil legal services lawyers, paralegals, law students, social workers, and youth advocates from local universities and nonprofit organizations.

The materials from these training events include practice tips, copies of pertinent laws and regulations, checklists, forms, sample correspondence and pleadings, and information on resources and local contacts. The resulting "tool box" provides a practical "how to" approach to assist attorneys— particularly education advocates—in working collaboratively with the school system and other agencies responsible for delivering services to children with special needs.

PDS also compiles a Youth Resource Directory of services for youth involved with the juvenile justice system. Public defenders, guardians ad litem, social workers, and other practitioners can use the directory to find services for youth in their care. The directory is organized by type of service: acute psychiatric care, alternative living, drug education and treatment, educational and vocational training, medical and mental health services, monitoring programs, afterschool and mentoring programs, and other services. Three members of the PDS Offender Rehabilitation Division staff are experts in juvenile mental health and are available for consultation. Consultation is also available through the Division's Duty Day services.

In addition to the 8 to 12 defense attorneys in the PDS Juvenile Division, 2 PDS social workers focus exclusively on juvenile cases and assist with pretrial detention alternatives and long-term program development. PDS attorneys also represent juveniles in special education, child disability, and other civil matters that are related to (or collateral consequences of) delinquency proceedings. Two of the PDS special education attorney positions are funded through an award under OJJDP's Juvenile Accountability Block Grants (JABG) program. Thus, PDS has developed a "team defense" approach to ensure that juveniles receive quality defense, that education needs are recognized and responded to as available resources permit, and that children with special needs receive public benefits, social services, and community-based treatment services where appropriate.

In 1982, in response to concerns about incarcerated youth in need of legal guidance and access to counsel, PDS created the Juvenile Services Program (JSP) at Oak Hill Youth Center, the District's juvenile corrections facility. In 1999, JSP became a component of the PDS Community Defender Program. The JSP coordinator and staff attorney develop services beyond the gates of Oak Hill to help divert youth from the facility and meet the needs of youth who leave the facility for distant residential placements. JSP also works to facilitate reentry into the community for youth at Oak Hill and for children in any of the District's shelters. Under the JSP coordinator's supervision, the staff attorney trains and supervises law clerks, who work to ensure that the due process rights of incarcerated youth are protected at disciplinary hearings. Over the years, JSP has worked with thousands of incarcerated youth, but no definitive research has been conducted on the eventual outcomes for these youth. Recently, the Mayor's Blue Ribbon Commission on Youth Safety and Juvenile Justice voted to demolish Oak Hill and replace it with new facilities and more community-based programs for delinquents (Chan, 2001). PDS is monitoring these developments as it continues to offer legal services to preadjudicated, detained, incarcerated, and committed youth.

For additional information on PDS, contact:

Avis Buchanan
Director
Public Defender Service for the District of Columbia
633 Indiana Avenue NW.
Washington, DC 20001
202–628–1200
202–626–8423 (fax)

TeamChild

A majority of youth involved in the juvenile justice system are struggling with untreated mental illness, addiction, learning disabilities, and unsafe living environments. Many of these youth are disconnected from school, positive adults and peers, and stable homes. Once involved in the juvenile justice system, they drift further away and are often excluded altogether from community support. Many youth can be diverted from delinquency and violence if their basic needs are met. This basic premise underlies the work of TeamChild, a Washington-based civil legal advocacy project for youth involved in the juvenile justice system.

TeamChild goes to the roots of delinquency by providing civil legal advocacy and mentoring to young people who are having difficulty gaining access to education, treatment, and safe living situations. Public defenders, juvenile probation officers, community service providers, and courts refer youth to TeamChild for representation. As part of its unique relationship with youth, TeamChild actively engages them in problem solving, gives them a voice in planning for their future, and helps them develop the skills they need for adulthood and independence.

TeamChild has been proven to be a cost-effective approach to reducing recidivism in juveniles. A study done by the Washington State Institute for Public Policy showed that TeamChild saves taxpayers nearly $4,000 for each child receiving full services. TeamChild's holistic advocacy for youth has been recognized nationally and replicated around the country.

TeamChild was piloted in 1995 through a Title II Formula Grant from OJJDP. The project was born out of collaboration among Columbia Legal Services, the Seattle-King County Defender Association, and the Washington Defender Association. Since its creation, TeamChild has grown from a one-person office in Seattle to an organization with five offices and more than a dozen staff members helping hundreds of youth in five Washington counties. TeamChild's successful expansion over the past 8 years is built on a solid service delivery model that fills a critical need for communities struggling to support youth in trouble.

For additional information on TeamChild, contact:

Anne Lee
Executive Director
TeamChild
1120 East Terrace Street, Suite 203
Seattle, WA 98122
206–322–2444
206–381–1742 (fax)
anne.lee@teamchild.org

Youth Advocacy Project

The Youth Advocacy Project (YAP), Roxbury, MA, was founded in 1992 by the Committee for Public Counsel Services, the public defender office for the Commonwealth of Massachusetts. YAP's initial mission was limited to defending indigent juveniles charged with serious criminal offenses and who faced the possibility of incarceration in an adult facility. The mission was later broadened to encompass the underlying issues that contribute to juvenile offending. In 1993, YAP began to represent youth charged with lesser offenses and to offer expanded advocacy and other intervention services.

YAP's primary function is to provide comprehensive legal representation and advocacy for youth charged as delinquent and youthful offenders in Boston's juvenile courts. In 1999–2000, YAP attorneys handled 820 delinquency and youthful offender cases involving 525 youth. YAP offers clinical assessments, service planning, referrals, and social services consultation to high-risk youth. It also works with youth in disciplinary and administrative proceedings, including school suspension and expulsion hearings, special education meetings, and Department of Youth Services conferences. Although YAP services are available to youth ages 7–21 throughout Boston, its constituency comes primarily from the predominantly African American neighborhoods of Dorchester and Roxbury. Most youth receiving direct legal services are boys; equal numbers of boys and girls receive prevention services.

The Committee for Public Counsel Services' 15-person oversight committee, which is appointed by the Massachusetts Supreme Judicial Court, oversees YAP. The YAP staff includes a director, one supervising attorney, two social workers, a psychologist, a community liaison, a Know the Law workshop coordinator, and an administrative assistant. Staff members are often assisted by law students, graduate students of social work and public health, and undergraduate interns.

YAP is intensively involved in community efforts and outreach. It has offered several hundred training sessions on a variety of juvenile justice issues for attorneys and youth services professionals and has conducted 700 Know the Law workshops for more than 10,000 participants. The Roxbury Network and the Dudley Outreach Workers Network are partnerships between YAP and more than a dozen Roxbury youth-serving agencies. The goals of the networks are to maximize the use of existing resources, work collaboratively to improve existing services and implement new ones, and develop a strategy for long-term systemic change (Youth Advocacy Project, 2000a; 2000b). YAP also publishes a Community Notebook designed to assist lawyers, probation officers, staff in the Department of Youth Services and Department of Social Services, and other youth workers in understanding the needs of their clients and identifying community resources available to meet those needs.

In partnership with the Children's Law Center of Massachusetts, Inc., YAP launched the EdLaw Project in January 2000. The project was based on local research showing that nearly 80 percent of YAP's delinquency clients experienced school failure prior to court involvement and on national research indicating that lack of appropriate academic achievement is the leading indicator for chronic court involvement. The EdLaw Project advocates for appropriate education services for Boston's high-risk children, addressing such issues as academic failure, suspension and expulsion, undetected special needs, inadequate education while in state custody, and reintegration in the school system following detention or incarceration. The project has grown to include three attorneys and, in addition to direct advocacy work, has partnered with local residents and agencies, such as La Alianza Hispana, Parents Place, the Center for Law and Education, and the Boston Parents Organizing Network, to deliver a variety of workshops and conferences for parents and youth workers on parental engagement, parental rights and responsibilities, and the components of a quality standards-based education (Children's Law Center of Massachusetts, Inc., and Youth Advocacy Project, 2000).

In 2003, YAP created the Juvenile Defender Support Network. With the assistance of a JABG grant, YAP added two staff members to train and support the 375 solo practitioners who provide the bulk of the indigent defense services to court-involved children throughout Massachusetts.

YAP also hosts the Equal Justice Partnership (EJP), which consists of upper-level managers from most of the Commonwealth agencies involved in Massachusetts' juvenile justice system. The primary goal of EJP is to enhance the capacity of the juvenile court to promote healthy outcomes for court-involved youth by improving communication and collaboration among juvenile justice system stakeholders. EJP is developing a model job-readiness program for youth on probation, piloting a youth development assessment tool, and developing Youth Development Approach training curriculums for agencies that work with court-involved youth.

YAP funding comes from a variety of sources. The Massachusetts legislature is the largest supporter, but YAP also receives grants from foundations and private donors. Several foundations—Shaw, Public Welfare, Boston, Boston Bar, Massachusetts Bar, and Mifflin—have all provided substantial support over the past 10 years. The education advocacy initiative has received substantial support from several private donors and foundations, as well as from the City of Boston. The Hyams Foundation provided a 2-year grant for a coordinator position at La Alianza Hispana, a neighborhood organization that works with YAP in Roxbury's Hispanic community.

YAP has completed an external process evaluation of its services. It has also begun the process of designing an outcome evaluation.

For additional information on YAP, contact:

Joshua Dohan
Director
Youth Advocacy Project
10 Malcolm X Blvd.
Roxbury, MA 02119
617–445–5640
617–541–0904 (fax)
jdohan@publiccounsel.net

Remaining Challenges

It is evident from this review that several states are actively addressing the need to provide access to well-trained, experienced, and dedicated defense attorneys for indigent youth in the juvenile justice system. Several of the programs described offer training to help defense counsel learn more about working with youth. Integration of social services and education professionals into public defenders' offices, another feature of several programs, shows promise in addressing the service needs of youth who come in contact with the juvenile justice system. The use of volunteer community-based advocates, as implemented by the Mesa County (CO) Partners, shows promise in involving families, ensuring that youth appear in court as scheduled, and reducing recidivism.

Nevertheless, as indicated by the national and state-level research cited, many important challenges remain to be addressed before juvenile defendants can count on receiving effective legal counsel to protect their rights to due process and fair treatment in the juvenile justice system. Unfortunately, until compensation and working conditions improve, the early exodus of juvenile defense attorneys from the field is likely to continue. Without more skillful, consistent, and zealous representation, too many youthful offenders will be placed in more restrictive settings than appropriate and will not receive critical services. States and counties should address these challenges in meaningful ways, affording the juvenile defense bar the recognition it deserves and providing first-class resources that enable attorneys to do their jobs well.

Resource Organizations

National Association of Criminal Defense Lawyers

The National Association of Criminal Defense Lawyers (NACDL) is the preeminent organization advancing the mission of the nation's criminal defense lawyers to ensure justice and due process for persons accused of crime or other misconduct. It is a professional bar association that includes private criminal defense lawyers, public defenders, military defense counsel, law professors, and judges. The organization tracks legislation and publishes news articles related to defense and indigent defense issues.

For additional information on NACDL, visit the Web site at www.nacdl.org or contact:

National Association of Criminal Defense Lawyers
1150 18th Street NW., Suite 950
Washington, DC 20036
202–872–8600
202–872–8690 (fax)
assist@nacdl.org

National Juvenile Defender Center

Created in 1991 with support from OJJDP and private foundations, the National Juvenile Defender Center is dedicated to building the capacity of the juvenile defense bar and improving access to counsel and quality of representation for children in delinquency and criminal proceedings. The center provides juvenile defense attorneys with a forum for addressing practice issues, improving advocacy skills, building partnerships, exchanging information, and participating in the national debate about juvenile crime. Through its central office in Washington, DC, and nine regional affiliates, the center offers training and technical assistance, advocacy, networking, collaboration, capacity building, and coordination services. The center is managed by the American Bar Association Juvenile Justice Center, in partnership with the Youth Law Center and the Juvenile Law Center.

For additional information on the National Juvenile Defender Center, visit the Web site at www.abanet.org/crimjust/juvjus/jdc.html or contact:

Patricia Puritz, J.D.
National Juvenile Defender Center
740 15th Street NW., 7th Floor
Washington, DC 20005
202–662–1506
202–662–1507 (fax)
juvjus@staff.abanet.org

National Legal Aid & Defender Association

The National Legal Aid & Defender Association (NLADA) is an advocacy organization representing legal aid and defender programs and individual advocates. It is the oldest and largest national, nonprofit membership association devoted entirely to serving the equal justice community. NLADA conducts training for defense attorneys in general, with some training geared specifically to juvenile defenders. It compiles resources and publications and provides technical assistance to attorneys and other groups interested in civil legal aid and indigent criminal defense.

For additional information on NLADA, visit the Web site at www.nlada.org or contact:

National Legal Aid & Defender Association
1140 Connecticut Avenue NW., Suite 900
Washington, DC 20036
202–452–0620
202–872–1031 (fax)
info@nlada.org

Useful Tools

Compendium of Standards

Compendium of Standards for Indigent Defense Systems: A Resource Guide for Practitioners and Policymakers. Volume V: Standards for Juvenile Justice Defense (U.S. Bureau of Justice Assistance, 2000) brings together the IJA-ABA *Juvenile Justice Standards* published in 1980 and standards and guidelines issued by public defender commissions in Connecticut, Indiana, Massachusetts, Minnesota, North Dakota, and Washington.

The compendium is available online at www.ojp.usdoj.gov/indigentdefense/compendium/pdftxt/vol5.pdf. A CD–ROM may be ordered through the Bureau of Justice Assistance (BJA) Clearinghouse by the following methods:

E-mail: puborder@ncjrs.org.
Phone: 800–851–3420
Mail: BJA Clearinghouse, P.O. Box 6000, Rockville, MD 20849–6000.

Delinquency Notebook

The ABA Juvenile Justice Center has published the *Juvenile Defender Delinquency Notebook* (Butterworth, Ree, and Scali, 2000), a case management and preparation system that offers attorneys who are new to the juvenile justice process a step-by-step guide to defending a juvenile case. The *Notebook* includes law and procedure checklists, trial preparation and strategy forms, model forms and motions, and summaries of key trial documents. It also includes the IJA-ABA *Juvenile Justice Standards* and a list of resources.

For additional information on the *Delinquency Notebook*, contact:

American Bar Association Juvenile Justice Center
740 15th Street NW., 10th Floor
Washington, DC 20005
202–662–1506
202–662–1501 (fax)
juvjus@abanet.org

From Promising Programs

Public Defender Service for the District of Columbia. Materials available from PDS include its Youth Resource Directory and special education advocacy training "toolbox" (for descriptions and contact information, see page 23). The PDS Web site (pdsdc.org) offers a calendar of upcoming training and other events, a "virtual attorney" for posting legal questions, descriptions of PDS services, and links to related Web sites.

First Defense Legal Aid. "Train the trainers" materials are available from FDLA (for description and contact information, see page 20).

Legislation

State laws relevant to indigent defense can be located through Findlaw.com, a free Internet service.

References

Albin, B., Albin, M., Gladden, E., Ropelato, S., and Stoll, G. 2003. *Montana: An Assessment of Access to Counsel and Quality of Representation in Delinquency Proceedings*. Washington, DC: American Bar Association Juvenile Justice Center.

American Bar Association. 2002. *ABA Model Rules of Professional Conduct*. Chicago, IL: American Bar Association.

American Bar Association Juvenile Justice Center and New England Juvenile Defender Center. 2003. *Maine: An Assessment of Access to Counsel and Quality of Representation in Delinquency Proceedings*. Washington, DC: American Bar Association Juvenile Justice Center.

Black, H.C., and Garner, B.A., eds. 2000. *Black's Law Dictionary, Abridged,* 7th ed. Eagan, MN: West Group.

Brooks, K., and Kamine, D. 2003. *Justice Cut Short: An Assessment of Access to Counsel and Quality of Representation in Delinquency Proceedings in Ohio*. Washington, DC: American Bar Association Juvenile Justice Center.

Burruss, G., and Kempf-Leonard, K. 2000. *Attorney Representation and Impact in Serious Delinquency Cases: An Evaluation of Three Missouri Circuits*. St. Louis, MO: University of Missouri-St. Louis, Department of Criminology and Criminal Justice.

Butterworth, B., Rhee, W., and Scali, M.A., eds. 2000. *Juvenile Defender Delinquency Notebook*. Washington, DC: American Bar Association Juvenile Justice Center.

Butts, J.A. 1994. *Offenders in Juvenile Court 1992*. Bulletin. U.S. Department of Justice, Office of Justice Programs, Office of Juvenile Justice and Delinquency Prevention.

Calvin, E. 2003. *Washington: An Assessment of Access to Counsel and Quality of Representation in Delinquency Proceedings*. Washington, DC: American Bar Association Juvenile Justice Center.

Celeste, G., ed. 2001. *The Children Left Behind: An Assessment of Access to Counsel and Quality of Representation in Delinquency Proceedings in Louisiana*. New Orleans, LA: Juvenile Justice Project of Louisiana.

Chan, S. 2001. Panel proposes leveling Oak Hill. *Washington Post* (August 29):B3.

Chase, T., and Gonnell, F. 2003. *Law School Debt and the Practice of Law*. New York, NY: Association of the Bar of the City of New York.

Children's Law Center of Massachusetts, Inc., and Youth Advocacy Project. 2000. *EdLaw Project 2000 Annual Report*. Lynn, MA: Children's Law Center of Massachusetts; Roxbury, MA: Youth Advocacy Project.

Clark, B. 2001. The American Bar Association National Juvenile Defender Center. Presentation at the Coalition for Juvenile Justice Conference, Washington, DC, March 30, 2001.

Colorado Department of Public Safety. 2000. Colorado FY 2000–2002 multi-year comprehensive juvenile justice and delinquency prevention state plan. Unpublished document. Denver, CO: Colorado Department of Public Safety, Division of Criminal Justice.

Cooper, N.L., Puritz, P., and Shang, W. 1998. Fulfilling the promise of *In Re Gault:* Advancing the role of lawyers for children. *Wake Forest Law Review* 33(3):651–679.

Cumming, E., Finley, M., Hall, S., Humphrey, A., and Picou, I. 2003. *Maryland: An Assessment of Access to Counsel and Quality of Representation in Delinquency Proceedings*. Washington, DC: American Bar Association Juvenile Justice Center.

Dorfman, L., and Schiraldi, V. 2001. *Off Balance: Youth, Race & Crime in the News*. Washington, DC: Youth Law Center, Building Blocks for Youth.

Equal Justice Works, National Association for Law Placement, and Partnership for Public Service. 2002. *From Paper Chase to Money Chase: Law School Debt Diverts Road to Public Service*. Washington, DC. Equal Justice Works, National Association for Law Placement, and Partnership for Public Service.

Fritsch, J., and Rohde, D. 2001. Legal help often fails New York's poor. *New York Times* (April 8):1.

Greene, R., and Dougherty, G. 2001. Kids in prison: Young inmates report highest rate of assault. *Miami Herald* (March 19):1A.

Grindall, L. 2003. *North Carolina: An Assessment of Access to Counsel and Quality of Representation in Delinquency Proceedings*. Washington, DC: American Bar Association Juvenile Justice Center.

Harms, P. *Detention in Delinquency Cases, 1990–1999*. 2003. Fact Sheet. Washington, DC: U.S. Department of Justice, Office of Justice Programs, Office of Juvenile Justice and Delinquency Prevention.

Hawkins, D.F., Laub, J.H., Lauritsen, J.L., and Cothern, L. 2000. *Race, Ethnicity, and Serious and Violent Juvenile Offending*. Bulletin. Washington, DC: U.S. Department of Justice, Office of Justice Programs, Office of Juvenile Justice and Delinquency Prevention.

Henry, D.A. 1999. *Pathways to Juvenile Detention Reform. 5. Reducing Unnecessary Delay: Innovations in Case Processing*. Baltimore, MD: The Annie E. Casey Foundation.

Illinois Department of Human Services. 2000. Illinois FY 2000–2002 multi-year comprehensive juvenile justice and delinquency prevention state plan. Unpublished document. Chicago, IL: Illinois Department of Human Services, Office of Prevention.

Institute for Judicial Administration-American Bar Association (IJA-ABA). 1980. *Juvenile Justice Standards.* Washington, DC: American Bar Association.

Leiber, M.J., and Stairs, J.M. 1999. Race, contexts, and the use of intake diversion. *Journal of Research in Crime and Delinquency* 36(1):56–86.

Luczycki, R. 2003. Starting salaries level off. *National Jurist* 13(2):28.

Miller-Wilson, L.S. 2003. *Pennsylvania: An Assessment of Access to Counsel and Quality of Representation in Delinquency Proceedings.* Washington, DC: American Bar Association Juvenile Justice Center.

National Council of Juvenile and Family Court Judges. 2001. *Establishing Juvenile Drug Courts: A Judicial Curriculum.* Reno, NV: National Council of Juvenile and Family Court Judges.

New York Legal Aid Society. 2000. *Annual Report 2000.* New York, NY: New York Legal Aid Society.

Poe-Yamagata, E., and Jones, M.A. 2000. *And Justice for Some: Differential Treatment of Minority Youth in the Justice System.* Washington, DC: Youth Law Center, Building Blocks for Youth.

Puritz, P., and Brooks, K. 2002. *Kentucky: Advancing Justice: An Assessment of Access to Counsel and Quality of Representation in Delinquency Proceedings.* Washington, DC: American Bar Association Juvenile Justice Center.

Puritz, P., Burrell, S., Schwartz, R., Soler, M., and Warboys, L. 1995. *A Call for Justice: An Assessment of Access to Counsel and Quality of Representation in Delinquency Proceedings.* Washington, DC: American Bar Association Juvenile Justice Center.

Puritz, P., Scali, M., and Picou, I. 2002. *Virginia: An Assessment of Access to Counsel and Quality of Representation in Delinquency Proceedings.* Washington, DC: American Bar Association Juvenile Justice Center.

Puritz, P., and Sun, T. 2001. *Georgia: An Assessment of Access to Counsel and Quality of Representation in Delinquency Proceedings.* Washington, DC: American Bar Association Juvenile Justice Center.

Puzzanchera, C. 2003. *Delinquency Cases Waived to Criminal Court, 1990–1999.* Fact Sheet. Washington, DC: U.S. Department of Justice, Office of Justice Programs, Office of Juvenile Justice and Delinquency Prevention.

Redding, R. 2003. The effects of sentencing juveniles as adults: Research and policy implications. *Youth Violence and Juvenile Justice* 1(2):28–55.

Shepherd, R.E., Jr. 1998. *Criminal Justice.* Washington, DC: American Bar Association.

Stahl, A.L. 2003. *Delinquency Cases in Juvenile Courts, 1999.* Fact Sheet. Washington, DC: U.S. Department of Justice, Office of Justice Programs, Office of Juvenile Justice and Delinquency Prevention.

Stanfield, R. 1999. *Pathways to Juvenile Detention Reform. Overview. The JDAI Story.* Baltimore, MD: The Annie E. Casey Foundation.

Steinberg, L. 2003. Juveniles on trial, MacArthur Foundation study calls competency into question. *Criminal Justice* 18(3):21. Washington, DC: American Bar Association.

Stewart, C.E., Celeste, G., Marrus, E., Picou, I., Puritz, P., and Utter, D. 2000. *Selling Justice Short, Juvenile Indigent Defense in Texas.* Austin, TX: Texas Appleseed.

U.S. Bureau of Justice Assistance. 2000. *Compendium of Standards for Indigent Defense Systems: A Resource Guide for Practitioners and Policymakers. Volume V: Standards for Juvenile Justice Defense.* Washington, DC: U.S. Department of Justice, Office of Justice Programs, Bureau of Justice Assistance.

U.S. Government Accounting Office. 1995. *Juvenile Justice Representation Rates Varied as Did Counsel's Impact on Court Outcomes.* GAO/GGD–95–139. Washington, DC: U.S. Government Accounting Office.

Young, M.C. 2000. *Providing Effective Representation for Youth Prosecuted as Adults.* Washington, DC: U.S. Department of Justice, Office of Justice Programs, Bureau of Justice Assistance.

Young, M.C., and Gainsborough, J. 2000. *Prosecuting Juveniles in Adult Court: An Assessment of Trends and Consequences.* Washington, DC: The Sentencing Project.

Youth Advocacy Project. 2000a. *Fact Sheet.* Roxbury, MA: Youth Advocacy Project.

Youth Advocacy Project. 2000b. *1990–2000 Annual Report.* Roxbury, MA: Youth Advocacy Project.

Acknowledgments

This Bulletin was written by Judith B. Jones, M.A., Spec. H.S.A. Ms. Jones expects to receive her J.D. degree from the Catholic University of America Columbus School of Law in 2005.

This Bulletin was prepared under Contract number OJP–2000–298–BF with the Office of Juvenile Justice and Delinquency Prevention.

Points of view or opinions expressed in this document are those of the author and do not necessarily represent the official position or policies of OJJDP or the U.S. Department of Justice.

The Office of Juvenile Justice and Delinquency Prevention is a component of the Office of Justice Programs, which also includes the Bureau of Justice Assistance, the Bureau of Justice Statistics, the National Institute of Justice, and the Office for Victims of Crime.

NCJ 204063